Never Thirsty

Quenching Your Spiritual Thirst with Artistic Meditations on Scripture.

Artist and Author Julie R. Elroy

Never Thirsty
Quenching Your Spiritual Thirst with Artistic Meditations on Scripture.
By Julie R. Elroy

Contents

Forward

This book contains examples of my own meditations on Scripture. These meditations should not be a substitute for your own meditations, but a starting point and example of a meditation you can have of your own. The paintings may inspire you to remember the Scripture you have read so you can meditate on it throughout your day. After you have read the Scripture, try to put yourself in the scene from the Bible or possibly the character of the painting. Be alert and open to the message that the Holy Spirit has for you today. In your mind, try to imagine yourself as one or more of the characters in the Scripture. Questions will come to your mind. You may ask yourself questions like, "What would Jesus say to me?" Focus on finding the answers to these questions with the guidance of the Holy Spirit.

Words from the Artist

My paintings contained in this book were inspired through reading the Bible and listening to the Holy Spirit telling me what I need in my life. When I paint, it is my meditation time. I am open to what the Holy Spirit has to say to me. I hope the paintings that I share will be as meaningful to you as they were to me. Each painting is simple and focused. When I paint, I become the character in the painting. I hope you can envision yourself as the character as well.

The main theme throughout this book is feeding your Spiritual needs through reading the Scripture. The Scripture is like water that feeds a tree or cool water that can quench your thirst. We all have a Spiritual longing that can be filled through Christ Jesus. One of the ways we can experience spiritual growth is by having meditations on Scripture. I hope the scriptures mentioned in this book will encourage you to grow spiritually and to meditate. I hope the paintings in this book will touch your heart and cause you to search for the love of Jesus in your soul.

A few of the paintings in this book were signed under my maiden name Julie R. Sealock. As of March 25, 2000, my new name is Julie R. Elroy. I thank The Almighty Creator for giving me this talent and inspiration.

"Desert Flowers" ©1995
Oil, 24" x 20"

"Desert Flowers"

"The Lord will guide you continually, giving you water when you are dry and restoring your strength. You will be like a well-watered garden, like an ever-flowing spring" (NLT, Isaiah 58:11).

"You made all the delicate, inner parts of my body and knit me together in my mother's womb. Thank you for making me so wonderfully complex! Your workmanship is marvelous—how well I know it. You watched me as I was being formed in utter seclusion, as I was woven together in the dark of the womb. You saw me before I was born. Every day of my life was recorded in your book. Every moment was laid out before a single day had passed. How precious are your thoughts about me, O God. They cannot be numbered! I can't even count them; they outnumber the grains of sand! And when I wake up, you are still with me!"
(NLT, Psalm 139: 13-18).

"Let all that I am praise the LORD; may I never forget the good things he does for me" (NLT Psalm 103:2).

Like the desert, life can seem unbearable at times. Life can make me thirst for more. Like the Saguaro cactus waiting hundreds of years to show signs of maturity, I too wait for growth and change in myself. As the desert defends itself against the environment and the predator, Lord, I have your protection for my growth and beauty. The dry desert transforms into beautiful blooms after waiting decades for a drink of water. Lord, please help me wait for your timing. You will watch me bloom into the beautiful creation you have planned for my life. Help me to never take for granted the beautiful life you have given me to enjoy. Never thirsty.

"What Have I Done?" © 2021
Oil, 16" x 20"

"What Have I Done?"

"He is so rich in kindness and grace that he purchased our freedom with the blood of his Son and forgave our sins" (NLT, Ephesians 1:7).

"He forgives all my sins and heals all my diseases. He redeems me from death and crowns me with love and tender mercies. He fills my life with good things. My youth is renewed like the eagle's! The LORD is compassionate and merciful, slow to get angry and filled with unfailing love" (NLT, Psalm 103:3-5 and 8).

"He has removed our sins as far from us as the east is from the west. The LORD is like a father to his children, tender and compassionate to those who fear him. For he knows how weak we are; he remembers we are only dust" (NLT, Psalm 103:12-14).

"Wash me clean from my guilt. Purify me from my sin" (NLT, Psalm 51:2).

I go to the tomb of Christ to meditate. Jesus' head rests on my lap. Oh, sweet Jesus, what have I done? I see your broken, bruised and battered body. You have taken the punishment that I deserve. Forgive me. Give me the strength to forgive myself and to forgive others. On the third day, you arose from the grave. You help me to rise above my circumstances with your love, and grace. Being here in the tomb, I reflect on my need for forgiveness. I need a resurrection as well to rise up from my guilt and shame. Jesus, you give me hope. You change me into a new creation, totally cleansed. I stand up and leave this tomb. I walk out of the darkness of this tomb and into the light of day. This action reminds me of your forgiveness and being new again. Forgiven.

"Galatians 2:20" © 1996
Wire, wood, 8.5" x 6.5" x 8"

"Galatians 2:20"

"My old self has been crucified with Christ. It is no longer I who live, but Christ lives in me. So I live in this earthly body by trusting in the Son of God, who loved me and gave himself for me" (NLT, Galatians 2:20).

As I carry the cross, I look down and see the bloody tracks of crosses that have been carried before me. I reflect how the perfect Son of God was the sacrifice for all people. People in the past, present, and future. My skin is now stained by the blood of Christ that remained on the cross that I carry for Him. How do I carry this burden? How do I show Christ's love to others? What sacrifices do I need to make in order to help others? What sins do I need to nail to this cross? How do others see me? Do they see me as a servant of others? This path is difficult, but God gives me the strength to complete the task, the service, the difficult time. I must complete the plan God has for me. The reward comes later.

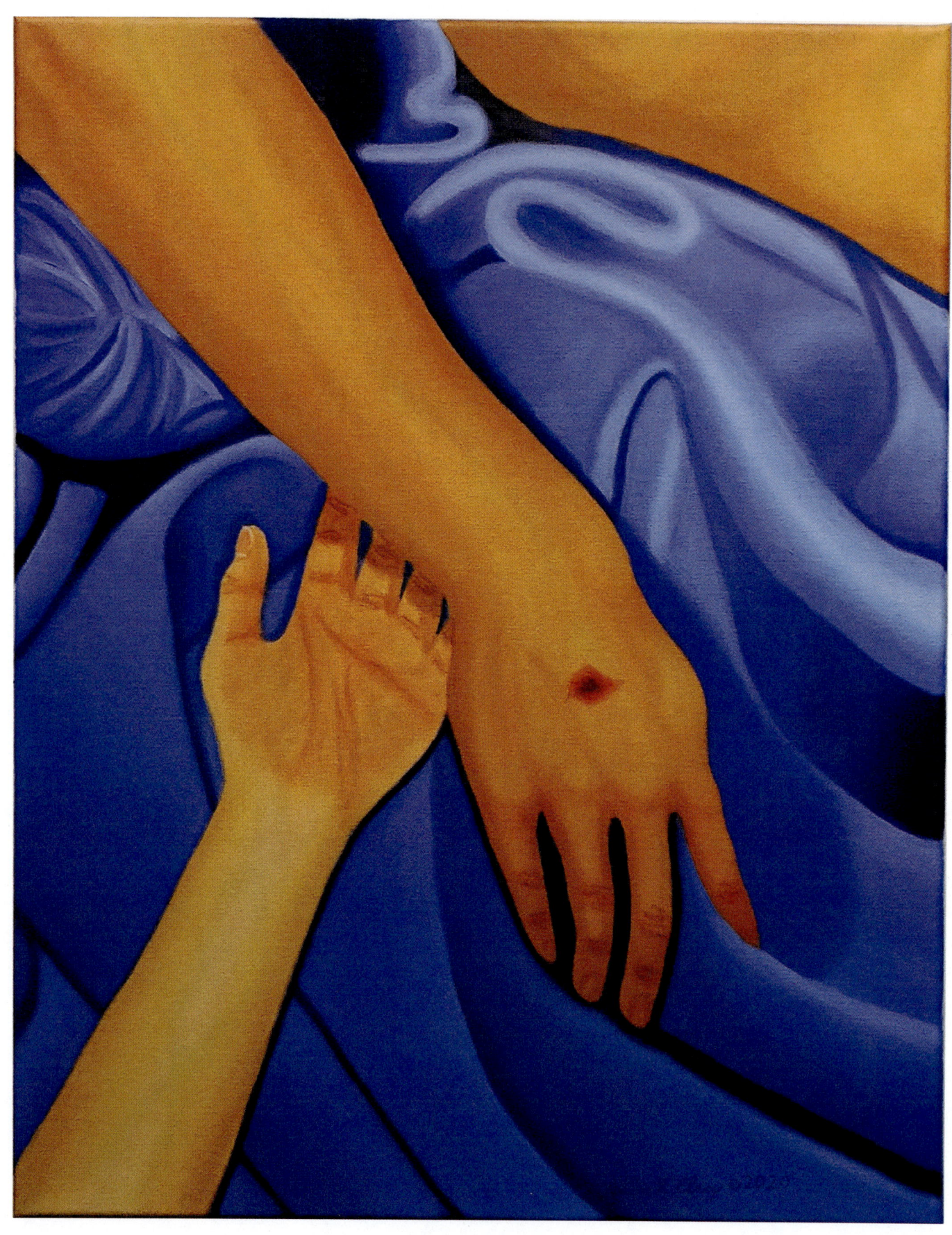

"Experiencing the Pieta" © 2020
Oil, 24" x 16"

"Experiencing the Pieta"

"And the Holy Spirit helps us in our weakness. For example, we don't know what God wants us to pray for. But the Holy Spirit prays for us with a groaning that cannot be expressed in words" (NLT, Romans 8:26).

"And then at last, the sign that the Son of Man is coming will appear in the heavens, and there will be deep mourning among all the peoples of the earth. And they will see the Son of Man coming on the clouds of heaven with power and great glory" (NLT Matthew 24:30).

I picture myself walking around Michelangelo's sculpture called, "Pieta". I participate in the sculpture by reaching out to the lifeless arm of Jesus. His hand is dangling down from Mother Mary's lap. How must Mary feel? How does God feel after watching His Son die and suffer this terrible death? The small lifeless body of Christ is draped over her lap to show the feeling of loss for her child. Mary must be thinking, "What did they do to my son?" She also realized He was God's Son. He was here for a short time for an important purpose; to be our Savior. Mary can manage her grief. She knows in her heart she will see Him again. Jesus overcame the grave. Jesus healed many people before rising up into heaven. I lay my burdens at His feet in prayer. Someday, He will come again. How can you have joy after grief? The answer is in the name of Jesus.

"Experiencing the Trinity" © 2020
Oil, 16" x 20"

"Experiencing the Trinity"

"And I will ask the Father, and he will give you another Advocate, who will never leave you. He is the Holy Spirit, who leads into all truth. The world cannot receive him, because it isn't looking for him and doesn't recognize him. But you know him, because he lives with you now and later will be in you" (NLT, John 14:16-17).

"For the glory of your name, O LORD, preserve my life. Because of your faithfulness, bring me out of this distress" (NLT, Psalm 143:11).

"Don't be afraid, for I am with you. Don't be discouraged, for I am your God. I will strengthen you and help you. I will hold you up with my victorious right hand" (NLT, Isaiah 41:10).

"For I know the plans I have for you," says the LORD. "They are plans for good and not for disaster, to give you a future and a hope" (NLT, Jeremiah 29:11).

I am sitting in my life boat. The waves rise and fall all around me. The waves are the struggles of my life. The cold wind howls all around me. The storms come and make me feel lost, confused, and alone. The boat rocks about and I am cold and wet. I sit on the lap of the Great Comforter, the Holy Spirit. He wraps his love around me like a blanket. The Holy Spirit comforts me and gives me peace. There ahead of me, I see God steering the boat. God knows the course of my life and the path I need to be on. I know He is in control of my life. Even when storms come and make me feel lost and alone, I trust in Him. I lean on Him in my difficult time. Sometimes I feel I need a rescue from the circumstances in my life. Just outside the boat, I see Jesus. He holds my hand through it all. Sometimes He asks me to come out and walk on the rough waters with Him. Do I have the faith to begin walking towards Him on the rough waters? I look out at the sunset. The storm is passing. This rough time in my life will also pass. The Trinity is with me through it all.

"I'm Coming!" © 2019
Oil, 20" x 16"

"I'm Coming!"

"But if we confess our sins to him, he is faithful and just to forgive us our sins and to cleanse us from all wickedness" (NLT, I John 1:9).

"My sheep listen to my voice; I know them, and they follow me. I give them eternal life, and they will never perish. No one can snatch them away from me, for my Father has given them to me, and he is more powerful than anyone else. No one can snatch them from the Father's hand. The Father and I are one" (NLT, John 10:27-30).

"Now may the God of peace— who brought up from the dead our Lord Jesus, the great Shepherd of the sheep, and ratified an eternal covenant with his blood— may he equip you with all you need for doing his will. May he produce in you, through the power of Jesus Christ, every good thing that is pleasing to him. All glory to him forever and ever! Amen" (NLT, Hebrews 13:20-21).

I need a rescue. I got lost and went the wrong way in life. I want Jesus to burst in and get me out of this difficult time. There is nothing too high, deep, or far for Jesus to come and save me. Why did I run away? The best place for me to be is in the arms of Jesus. Jesus, please forgive me. You took my punishment for me. I see your scars. You are much stronger now. You overcame the power of the grave. You came back to life on the third day. You want me to come back to your fold where it is safe. I think of the fold as heaven. Jesus, please forgive me. I was better off by your side all along. Bring me back to your fold. Jesus, I need your guidance daily. Thank you for rescuing me from this sin. I can't make it on my own. Thank you for your relentless love.

"Take That, Satan!" © 2022
Acrylic, 24" x 34"

"Take That, Satan!"

"All who do evil hate the light and refuse to go near it for fear their sins will be exposed. But those who do what is right come to the light so others can see that they are doing what God wants" (NLT, John 3 20-21).

"A final word: Be strong in the Lord and in his mighty power. Put on all of God's armor so that you will be able to stand firm against all strategies of the devil. For we are not fighting against flesh-and-blood enemies, but against evil rulers and authorities of the unseen world, against mighty powers in this dark world, and against evil spirits in the heavenly places. Therefore, put on every piece of God's armor so you will be able to resist the enemy in the time of evil. Then after the battle you will still be standing firm" (NLT, Ephesians 6:10-13).

"And the dragon was angry at the woman and declared war against the rest of her children—all who keep God's commandments and maintain their testimony for Jesus" (NLT, Revelation 12:17).

I see darkness all around me. Satan is looming like a dragon ready to strike. I tremble with fear of the unknown. I feel I am being attacked on all sides. Satan wants to destroy me. He wants me to lose my trust in God and reject the truth. Satan wants to mess up my life and prevent me from moving forward. I feel the heat of the fire all around me. Jesus is here with me. I am protected by His mighty power. I tell the fear that comes from Satan to hit the road. I will stand up to temptation. I am going to pray for my enemies. I am going to pray for the strength to forgive them. I'm going to let God heal my heart. Jesus has the power to cast out fear and give me strength. Jesus uses his majestic power to throw the fiery breath of Satan back into his evil face. Jesus will not let the enemy destroy me. Jesus is my super hero. Take that, Satan!

"Roots in the Rock" © 1996
Oil, 22" x 32"

"Roots in the Rock"

"He lets me rest in green meadows; he leads me beside peaceful streams" *(NLT, Psalm 23:2).*

"And now, just as you accepted Christ Jesus as your Lord, you must continue to follow him. Let your roots grow down into him, and let your lives be built on him. Then your faith will grow strong in the truth you were taught, and you will overflow with thankfulness" *(NLT, Colossians 2:6-7).*

"But blessed are those who trust in the Lord and have made the LORD their hope and confidence. They are like trees planted along a riverbank, with roots that reach deep into the water. Such trees are not bothered by the heat or worried by long months of drought. Their leaves stay green, and they never stop producing fruit" *(NLT, Jeremiah 17:7-8).*

I see the tree as a symbol of my spiritual life. The tree grows strong from the nourishment. The nourishment is the Word of God. The tree trunk and branches are strong enough to endure the winds and storms of life. The roots grow down into the rock which is the foundation. The foundation is strong because my faith has been growing stronger all along. The tree pulls water up by the roots. The water travels up through the tree trunk, and up through the branches. It moves on through the leaves, and on through the veins in the leaves. Then the water goes out into the air again. I must do the same with the Good News of Jesus Christ. I need to draw up nourishment, then spread God's love to the people throughout the world.

"Beauty by the Roadside No. 2" @ 1997
Watercolor, 15" x 22"

"Beauty by the Roadside No. 2"

"Don't you realize that your body is the temple of the Holy Spirit, who lives in you and was given to you by God? You do not belong to yourself, for God bought you with a high price. So you must honor God with your body"
(NLT, I Corinthians 6:19-20).

"And we know that God causes everything to work together for the good of those who love God and are called according to his purpose for them"
(NLT, Romans 8:28).

I take a walk and notice what is around me. I see an old rusty can on the ground. I look into the rusty can and find a beautiful flower. I reflect on how I see myself. I take this time to look inside myself and see my beauty. God can make me beautiful on the inside. God will use the mess I am in and turn it into something good. God can take the broken pieces of my life and turn it into a masterpiece. God's timing isn't always my timing. I know He has a plan. I believe God can work though my life and He will continue His good work. I believe God is the great healer. He will heal my every hurt and wipe away every tear. God, you are the strength in my heart and my full portion. You hold my hand and encourage me to move forward. You guide me to the unknown. You are all that I need in life. I am yours, forever.

"Mountains" © 1995
Acrylic, 26" x 18"

"Mountains"

"I look up to the mountains— does my help come from there? My help comes from the LORD, who made heaven and earth! He will not let you stumble; the one who watches over you will not slumber. Indeed, he who watches over Israel never slumbers or sleeps. The LORD himself watches over you! The LORD stands beside you as your protective shade. The sun will not harm you by day, nor the moon at night. The LORD keeps you from all harm and watches over your life. The LORD keeps watch over you as you come and go, both now and forever" (NLT, Psalm 121).

I see the mighty works of your hand when I look up at the mountains. I know you have this great power, and you can help me with my every need. I feel the warm sun on my skin. You comfort and love me so. Your beautiful creation is all around me. You caused the large rocks to rise up out of the ground. You are so powerful. And yet, the small flowers have been created with your delicate care. You have created all of this for me to enjoy. Your creation is changing constantly. The beauty is endless. Thank you Lord for all of this.

"Leaves on Water" © 2017
Oil, 24" x 18"

"Leaves on Water"

"Jesus answered, 'Everyone who drinks this water will be thirsty again, but whoever drinks the water I give them will never thirst. Indeed the water I give them will become in them a spring of water welling up to eternal life.' The woman said to him, 'Sir, give me this water so that I won't get thirsty and have to keep coming here to draw water" (NLT, John 4:13-15).

Oh Lord, let the Scripture fill the cup of my soul until it overflows. When I read your Word, it is like a waterfall from the heavens to my spirit. Lord, let your water feed my roots. Help me to draw up this water in my tree trunk of faith. Help me to stand firm. Help me be a prayer warrior. Help me to pray for those who need you most. The Angels will send my prayer message to God even though I don't know what to say in my prayer. Help me to remember that I may not see what blessing you have for me today, but the day will come when I will look back and see how you were working in my life all along. Help me to keep coming to your well of wisdom. Help me to search deep in the scriptures for the water I need every day. Lord, may your word be like cool water to my lips. Quench my thirst.

"Tree of Faith" © 1998
Watercolor 8" x 10"

"Tree of Faith"

"For the word of God is alive and powerful. It is sharper than the sharpest two-edged sword, cutting between soul and spirit, between joint and marrow. It exposes our innermost thoughts and desires. Nothing in all creation is hidden from God. Everything is naked and exposed before his eyes, and he is the one to whom we are accountable. So then, since we have a great High Priest who has entered heaven, Jesus the Son of God, let us hold firmly to what we believe. This High Priest of ours understands our weaknesses, for he faced all of the same testing we do, yet he did not sin. So let us come boldly to the throne of our gracious God. There we will receive his mercy, and we will find grace to help us when we need it most" (NLT, Hebrews 4:12-16).

"Then these righteous ones will reply, 'Lord, when did we ever see you hungry and feed you? Or thirsty and give you something to drink? "And the King will say, 'I tell you the truth, when you did it to one of the least of these my brothers and sisters, you were doing it to me!' (NLT, Matthew 25:37 and 40).

Lord, when I read your word, I get chills. These verses are so powerful and meaningful. Help me to continue to quench my spiritual thirst with your word. Help me to grow in you. Prune my useless branches. Help me to keep reaching out to help others and share your love. Lord, help me to stand up for what I believe. Help me to be like Christ, by being kind, helpful, and generous. Help me to take my eyes off of myself, and see others through your eyes. We are all your creations and you love us all the same. Help me to use your example when it comes to my attitude of service for others. Guide me, show me your will, and give me wisdom. Your work in me will not be done until the day I die.

"He Shows Me the Heavens" © 2022
Acrylic, 16" x 20"

"He Shows Me the Heavens"

"Take delight in the LORD, and he will give you your heart's desires. Commit everything you do to the LORD. Trust him, and he will help you. He will make your innocence radiate like the dawn, and the justice of your cause will shine like the noonday sun" (NLT, Psalm 37:4-6).

"Before I formed you in the womb I knew you..." (NLT Jerimiah 1:5 a).

"When I consider your heavens, the work of your fingers, the moon and the stars, which you have set in place, what is mankind that you are mindful of them, human beings that you care for them?" (NLT, Psalm 8:3-5).

"...being confident of this, that he who began a good work in you will carry it on to completion until the day of Christ Jesus" (NLT, Philippians 1:6).

God, I admire the universe that you are continuing to create to this very day. The boundaries of your creation are endless. The size of your creation is unimaginable. I feel very small as I gaze at outer space. Even though you have created all of these things, I know you care about me. You have immeasurable love for me. I know that you know my heart and about my troubles. I lay my cares in your hand. You support me in my life. You know how hard I try. You know my struggles. If I were the only person in the universe and I needed salvation, I know that Jesus would die on the cross for me. I will delight in the Lord and He will make me shine.

"The Grand Creator" © 2018
Oil, 16" x 20"

"The Grand Creator"

"LORD, you alone are my inheritance, my cup of blessing. You guard all that is mine. The land you have given me is a pleasant land. What a wonderful inheritance! I will bless the LORD who guides me; even at night my heart instructs me. I know the LORD is always with me. I will not be shaken, for he is right beside me. No wonder my heart is glad, and I rejoice. My body rests in safety. For you will not leave my soul among the dead or allow your holy one to rot in the grave. You will show me the way of life, granting me the joy of your presence and the pleasures of living with you forever" (NLT, Psalm 16:5-11).

I look out at the Grand Canyon. I wonder how you created this vast canyon. Its greatness extends beyond what I can see from here. The power of your wind and water over time was used to form these beautiful and majestic shapes. I admire your workmanship. I look down at the snow I am sitting on. Each flake is unique. You took the time to create each one. I have to take a magnifying glass or a microscope to enjoy the intricate details that each one carries. Just like the snowflakes, people have intricate differences that you carefully planned for us. As night falls over the canyon, and I see the stars. The stars are so far away, yet bright enough for me to enjoy their beauty. Lord, at times you feel so far away from me, yet all around I see the evidence that you are real, you are near, and I feel your love. I am so grateful and blessed.

"Moving Emotions No. 2." @1995
Oil, 36" x 30"

"Moving Emotions No. 2"

"Meanwhile, the disciples were in trouble far away from land, for a strong wind had risen, and they were fighting heavy waves. About three o'clock in the morning Jesus came toward them, walking on the water. When the disciples saw him walking on the water, they were terrified. In their fear, they cried out, "It's a ghost!" But Jesus spoke to them at once. "Don't be afraid," he said. "Take courage. I am here!" Then Peter called to him, "Lord, if it's really you, tell me to come to you, walking on the water." "Yes, come," Jesus said. So Peter went over the side of the boat and walked on the water toward Jesus. But when he saw the strong wind and the waves, he was terrified and began to sink. "Save me, Lord!" he shouted. Jesus immediately reached out and grabbed him. "You have so little faith," Jesus said. "Why did you doubt me?" When they climbed back into the boat, the wind stopped. Then the disciples worshiped him. "You really are the Son of God!" they exclaimed" (NLT, Mathew 14: 24-33).

I'm sitting in my life boat. The Holy Spirit wraps around me like a blanket. The Holy Spirit is my Great Comforter. My hands grip the boat. My knuckles are white from my grip. The boat is like a roller coaster as I ride the waves. The storm is crashing around me. The wind is howling so loud I can't think. The rain is cold on my face.

There in the gloomy distance is a yellow glow. The glow is getting closer. I see now that it is Jesus walking on the water. He commands the storm to be quiet. He tells the waves to be still. Jesus comes to my life boat and says to me, "Come. Walk with me on the water." I look down at my hands still white from my grip. I say "But Jesus, I'm scared!" I look at Jesus. He has a look of shock on His face that fills my heart with shame and guilt. Do I have the faith to get out of this boat? This small boat doesn't really provide any safety. Jesus says, "Don't you trust me?" Yes. I must step out of the boat and embrace the power of God. I need to break through this difficult time in my life. I receive His comfort and know that if I ask, He will answer my prayers. I am safe by His side. I take His hand and stand beside Him. I look out on the waters. The whole world seems to have gone mad. I share my heart with Jesus. I wrap my arms around Jesus like a child asking to be carried.

Jesus says, "Trust me, I will give you the power to forgive. I will cool your anger. I will heal your wounds. I will wipe away your tears."

I ask Jesus to cleanse my heart and to give me peace and joy. I ask Him to help me spread the Good News of Jesus Christ. I ask Him to give me a child-like faith. Jesus is my cornerstone.

Julie R. Elroy

Healing Touch

for Mind, Body, and Soul

An Artistic Look
at the
Healing Touches
of Jesus

Artist and Author Julie R. Elroy

Julie Elroy is an Author and Artist from Illinois, USA. If you have enjoyed this book, you may also enjoy Julie Elroy's first book called, "Healing Touch for Mind, Body, and Soul; An Artistic Look at the Healing Touches of Jesus." In this book you will find her beautiful paintings along with her personal interpretations of them. This book has further meditations on Scripture. This book also mentions Hymns that you may want to use for your music therapy, meditation, and worship.

Special Thanks

I thank The Almighty Creator for giving me this talent and inspiration. God's Word is nourishment to my soul. I want to continue to use my talent to further spread God's love through Jesus Christ.

I want to thank my loving husband for encouraging me in my love for art. With the help of family, we built our house by ourselves. We are so blessed to have two children that are so smart and healthy.

I want to thank my parents for encouraging me and supporting my talent. They also helped me to build a firm foundation of faith. With this foundation, my faith is now strong enough to endure the storms of life.

I want to thank my Mother-and Father-in-Law. They have shown me love and encouragement. They supported us with the joy of our children.

Made in the USA
Columbia, SC
02 May 2023

16033222R00022